Daily
Manifestation
Journal For Men & Women

Affirmation Exercises and Tools to Attract Love, Wealth, Happiness, and Abundance

Leslie Leong

© Copyright 2021 - All rights reserved.

The content contained within this book may not be reproduced, duplicated or transmitted without direct written permission from the author or the publisher.

Under no circumstances will any blame or legal responsibility be held against the publisher, or author, for any damages, reparation, or monetary loss due to the information contained within this book, either directly or indirectly.

Legal Notice:
This book is copyright protected. It is only for personal use. You cannot amend, distribute, sell, use, quote or paraphrase any part, or the content within this book, without the consent of the author or publisher.

Disclaimer Notice:
Please note the information contained within this document is for educational and entertainment purposes only. All effort has been executed to present accurate, up to date, reliable, complete information. No warranties of any kind are declared or implied. Readers acknowledge that the author is not engaged in the rendering of legal, financial, medical or professional advice. The content within this book has been derived from various sources. Please consult a licensed professional before attempting any techniques outlined in this book.

By reading this document, the reader agrees that under no circumstances is the author responsible for any losses, direct or indirect, that are incurred as a result of the use of the information contained within this document, including, but not limited to, errors, omissions, or inaccuracies.

Table of Contents

Preface

Understanding the Universal Energy and the Law of Attraction ... 1

How to Adopt a More Positive Mindset ... 8

Becoming a Vibrational Match to Your Dreams ... 12

Speaking Your Dreams Into Existence ... 46

Speaking Your Dreams Into Existence - Techniques ... 49

    Future Self Journaling

    Gratitude Jar

    Intention-Setting

    Abundance Tracker

    Guided Meditation: Manifesting Your Dream Life

How to Properly Use Positive Affirmations ... 99

    The Power of Affirmations and Guided Meditations

        Affirmations for Self-Love

Gratitude Is a Lifestyle ... 104

    Gratitude Wall

    Affirmations for Gratitude

Set Yourself Up to a Happier, Wealthier, and Fulfilling Life ... 108

    Affirmations to Create Your Reality

    Manifest Your Happier Version

References ... 192

Books In This Series ... 194

About The Author ... 196

Preface

Daily Manifestation Journal For Men & Women is an inspiring and empowering guide to the law of attraction with practical exercises, tools, and rituals that you can use to manifest the life you have always wanted to live.

By giving you clear directions and showing the 'what,' 'how,' and 'why' of each technique and tool - the author guides you and takes you on a journey within to teach you how you can reconnect with your true power and align yourself with what you want to create in your life.

Inside this Daily Manifestation Journal, you will find:

- A variety of affirmations for manifestation exercises and techniques you can choose from
- A guided gratitude journal to write in
- Daily Affirmations for each exercise
- Journal prompts to inspire reflection and self-awareness
- A space you can use to practice expressive writing
- Tools and techniques on personal development
- Universal Laws + Law of Attraction
- Everyday gratitude book
- A positive daily affirmations journal for women & men

- Do consider leaving a review for this journal on Amazon

Understanding the Universal Energy and the Law of Attraction

You have a decision to make: You can either go through life and let it happen to you, or you can take ownership for your life and happiness, and deliberately create a life of which you are proud. What will you consciously choose?

You are energy in motion. We all are magnets attracting to us what we are. Every single one of your thoughts, beliefs, and feelings is creating the reality you are about to experience right now. It's not what you want that you attract, but rather, what you are. The energy you send out to the world is always reflected back at you. What do you want to manifest more of in your life? Are you making sure you are vibrating at the same energy as what you want in your reality?

That's exactly what the law of attraction is about. Pure energy circulating from the universe to you and vice-versa. It's a constant and endless exchange of energy that builds up everything we know on this planet and out of it. For the universe, there is no such thing as bad energy or good energy, what exists is pure energy vibrating at different frequencies.

We as humans and as logical and emotional beings are the ones to attach meaning to what happens to us. These meanings are only present in our minds, and each and every one of us will interpret the same experience in totally different ways from one another based on the feelings and emotions we experience at the time.

This is precisely the reason why we are the ones creating our own reality. Every one of us has the power to perceive our realities in a multitude of ways, and as so, we go through life seeing things from unique pairs of lenses: Our unique perspectives.

Everything created in the world was first created in the mind and then brought to our physical world through our actions. For us, humans, our feelings, emotions, and our actions, are what puts the universe's energy into motion.

Although the law of attraction is the most known universal law, it's far from being the only one. In fact, there are dozens of them, but some of the most important are:

The Law of Pure Potentiality

This law allows all of us to have pure divine potential. The law of pure potentiality is fully achieved when someone is able to live life in total peace, total harmony, great abundance, and balance. Our level of consciousness is the one thing that determines if we will achieve this state of living at our full potential.

To truly experience our full potential, we have to live life fully connected to our soul, our feelings, and intuition.

The Law of Divine Oneness

This law states that everything in the universe is
interconnected and intertwined. Everything one does
affect the others on a universal scale.
We are all one divine force.

The Law of Cause and Effect

Exactly because we are all one, everything we do will cause
an effect, not only on us, but on everything around us too.
That's the law that influences our future since everything
we do today will affect our tomorrow.

The Law of Compensation

This is the law that makes the energy you put out come back to you. Let's remember, though, that compensation comes in many different forms, and not exactly how you picture compensation to be in your mind.

That's the meaning that you, as humans, attach to the word compensation.
The universe only understands energy.

Once you make a decision, the universe conspires to make it happen
- Ralph Waldo Emerson

The Law of Rhythm

This one is purely about movement and about cycles. The universe happens in cycles, nature comes in seasons, and humans age. Everything in the universe has a specific rhythm and is always changing. This is the law that makes things in life temporary. Life itself is rhythmic, and as so, impermanence is the only constant.

As you can see, all of these laws together help us understand the extent to which everything in the universe works and flows in harmony, and it's just natural that if we all lived in accordance with them, our lives would be much more peaceful, happier, and fulfilling.

How to Adopt a More Positive Mindset

What amount of effort are you truly willing to put into creating the life you want?

As we have just discussed, you attract what you are, so deciding you want something, embracing it with all your soul, and taking inspired action to actually make it happen is the secret to meaningful manifestations.

A positive mindset doesn't mean not having bad days and being happy 24/7. A positive mindset means having a positive attitude for everything that happens in life. Life itself happens in cycles, right? So, embrace the cycles and live life knowing that everything is temporary. Embrace the whole of you, and not just what you consider beautiful about you. Your whole being is divine and is worthy of experiencing here on Earth all the joy, love, peace, calm, and everything else that is truly meaningful to you.

Having a positive mindset starts by accepting you as being you and truly being aware that you are here on Earth to feel whole. Let's not confuse feeling whole with accepting and settling for less than what makes you fully happy. If you are not happy, then you have a choice to make: Create your own happiness or live a miserable life. There is no other alternative - either you take responsibility for going after what fulfills you, or you make peace with the fact that you don't want to create your happy reality.

Law of cause and effect, remember?

You are capable of doing everything you set your mind to - you just have to decide to go do it.
- Yes, there will be days when you feel tired and unmotivated.
- Yes, there will be days you will be faced with setbacks and unpredictable situations.
- Yes, there will be days you will go through heartbreaks.
- Yes, there will be days in which you will think that the only option is to give up.
- Yes, there will be days people will be gone. You will cry. You will suffer. You will regret. You will feel lost and uncertain.

That's exactly when your positive mindset will play a crucial role in your whole future ahead.

If you decide to:
- Keep going
- Push through
- Rest and recharge
- Find meaning in challenges and setbacks
- Look for the magic in the world everywhere
- Believe in yourself
- Believe you are worthy of the life you desire
- Believe that you can and you will
- Take charge of your life
- Take responsibility for your own happiness
- Embrace your feelings and emotions
- Embrace your wholeness
- Accept that failure is the way to success
- Find joy and happiness in the small things in life
- Keep yourself curious and always learning new things
- Never settle

If you train your mind to think, act, and believe in all these ways, the universe has no other choice but to match your life to all this positive energy you are putting out. That's the law of compensation.

Affirmations For Positive Mindset

- I am one with the divine force and I am open to receiving all the abundance in the universe
- I am open to new and exciting experiences
- I am a loving being and I am open to divine love
- I am ready to notice all the good around me
- I am love and I radiate love to everyone around me
- I love myself
- I know I am ready to create a life I feel happy about
- I can and I will.

Becoming a Vibrational Match to Your Dreams

What reality do you want to create for yourself? Are you manifesting something right now? If you are, remember to speak your dreams into existence. Align your energy to what you are creating. Believe with all your heart that what you are manifesting is on its way and that the universe is always listening (because it is).

When speaking about your dreams, meditate and visualize them. Send out a message of trust, passion, and enthusiasm.

When it comes to speaking your desires into existence, not only should you do that through the many law-of-attraction tools available, but also throw your desires out there into the world by sharing your hopes and wishes with the right people. The more you spread your wishes into the world, the more the universe shows its power by moving the right people, situations, events, and circumstances towards you. This is what we call synchronicities. You will get astonished by the number of people you could meet that are somehow connected to your desires.

Be careful though with the nay-sayers and party-poopers. Learn to recognize them along your manifesting journey, so that you can protect not only your energy but also your dreams from negativity.

Keeping your vibration high is essential to aligning yourself with your dreams, and let's not forget that when you hold in your heart the vision you want to manifest, you must take inspired actions to bring your dreams into the physical world. Anything that you believe with your whole heart to be true in the realm of possibility, will be manifested in your physical reality once you keep inspired and align your actions with your intentions.

You may be wondering how you can become a vibrational match to what you want to manifest, right?

Basically, we can divide this process into three steps that are somehow interconnected and intertwined.
1. Believe wholeheartedly you are worthy of receiving and can manifest what you want.
2. Learn to deal with and regulate your emotions, so that you can achieve autonomy to bring yourself back to calm when needed.
3. Experience the good-feeling thoughts of your desire as if it were already in your reality.

Believing you are worthy of your desires is one of the most important aspects of manifestation. Curious, though, is that this is also one of the most common reasons preventing people from manifesting - because they deal with limiting beliefs and self-love/self-worth issues.

Dealing with low self-esteem makes people start having counterproductive and self-sabotaging behaviors, which in turn, stops them from becoming a vibrational match to their wishes and dreams. Thus, it's important to do the inner-work, reframe your negative beliefs, and transform them into more positive and empowering beliefs.

How can you be sure of what you truly believe on a more subconscious level?

More often than not, we think we are being positive and believing in what we want, but what really happens is that our limiting beliefs are in the way of our manifestations.

So, the first step towards finding out what your subconscious beliefs are to take a good look at your current situation in life and analyze in what areas of life you are feeling stuck or not seeing progression and growth. These are the areas in which you may hold limiting beliefs, and these are the exact areas on which you must work.

Let's start our journaling practice towards your deepest manifestations! Grab your favorite magical pen and start reflecting on your current life.

Journaling Task 1

Becoming a vibrational match to your dreams: Uncovering your limiting beliefs

List all the areas in your life you need/want improvement or feel stuck in

1.

The second step is reflecting on your answers and focusing on questions one, three, and four. These are the three questions that contain the hidden signs of your deepest limiting beliefs.

For instance, let's say that for question one you answered something like;

I believe I am stuck because I always feel bad when others are way ahead of me and already have achieved so much and I haven't.

This way of thinking clearly shows that you are comparing yourself and your journey to others around you, and that sends the universe a message of total lack. You are focusing your energy on what you don't have and consequently, your focus on what is missing in your life removes your focus on gratitude.

There is no way you can be grateful in life and at the same time focus on what you don't have. When you focus on gratitude, you automatically notice and focus on everything that is going right for you in your life, and on all the things you take time to appreciate and cherish.

What's the hidden limiting belief there?

You may believe that you are not enough, you are not smart enough, you are not beautiful enough, or even that you are not lucky enough.

Remove the focus on what you don't have and focus your energy on what you are grateful for at the moment.
There is a big difference between focusing on your manifestations from feelings of lack and focusing on them with passion and enthusiasm.

Do this activity for every area of life you think you are stuck in and practice uncovering the hidden limiting beliefs in each of them.

Now that you have already removed some hidden layers of your limiting beliefs, let's focus on the second step of the process towards becoming a vibrational match to your desires - dealing with and regulating your emotions.

This second journaling activity will require that you dedicate a bit more time and energy to start becoming conscious about your feelings and emotions.

- For this activity, you will need to carry your journal around with you wherever you go for one week straight.
- You will practice becoming aware of your emotional triggers and how you react to these situations.

The whole idea of this practice is to create awareness about your emotional state and train your brain to replace aimlessly reacting to situations with acting in alignment with what you truly want to manifest - being more intentional with your actions.

Journaling Task 2

*Becoming a vibrational match to your dreams:
Uncovering your emotional triggers*

For a whole week, you are going to pay attention to every situation that makes you feel out of alignment, overwhelmed, stressed, worried, annoyed, sad, or nervous.

Let's train your brain to catch yourself whenever you feel one of these feelings listed above. Catching yourself in the exact moment you are out of alignment gives you the power to stop, breathe deeply, and reframe your thoughts to something that will make you feel calmer.

Journaling Task 2

Day 1:
Date:

1, Every time that something happens and takes you away from your calm, count to 10, breathe deeply, grab your journal, sit somewhere quiet or isolated, and write your thoughts down. What makes you feel out of alignment, overwhelmed, stressed, worried, annoyed, sad, or nervous.

2. Reflect about what happened, why you got nervous/sad/anxious, how you reacted at first, and list all the feelings that came to you at the moment.

Journaling Task 2

3. Can you find any limiting belief hidden in all the reasons you listed?

4. Could you have reacted in a different way? What ways?

5. What would be the positive aspects of having reacted differently to what happened?

6. Go back to the list of feelings you felt at the moment the situation happened. Go through each feeling and try to recall what were you thinking at the exact moment you felt that?

Journaling Task 2

7. Out of this list you made, separate two feelings that you want to feel less of during the week. For instance, let's say you want to feel less angry during this week.

- What actions can you take to feel less angry? How can you feel calmer when you are angry? Pick one action and commit to doing it next time anger comes in.

- Do this exact same exercise for the two feelings you chose and keep yourself accountable during the week. Every time you are about to feel that feeling, take the action that will make you feel a bit better.

Journaling Task 2

Day 2:
Date:

1, Every time that something happens and takes you away from your calm, count to 10, breathe deeply, grab your journal, sit somewhere quiet or isolated, and write your thoughts down. What makes you feel out of alignment, overwhelmed, stressed, worried, annoyed, sad, or nervous.

2. Reflect about what happened, why you got nervous/sad/anxious, how you reacted at first, and list all the feelings that came to you at the moment.

Journaling Task 2

3. Can you find any limiting belief hidden in all the reasons you listed?

4. Could you have reacted in a different way? What ways?

5. What would be the positive aspects of having reacted differently to what happened?

6. Go back to the list of feelings you felt at the moment the situation happened. Go through each feeling and try to recall what were you thinking at the exact moment you felt that?

Journaling Task 2

7. Out of this list you made, separate two feelings that you want to feel less of during the week. For instance, let's say you want to feel less angry during this week.

- What actions can you take to feel less angry? How can you feel calmer when you are angry? Pick one action and commit to doing it next time anger comes in.

- Do this exact same exercise for the two feelings you chose and keep yourself accountable during the week. Every time you are about to feel that feeling, take the action that will make you feel a bit better.

Journaling Task 2

Day 3:
Date:

1, Every time that something happens and takes you away from your calm, count to 10, breathe deeply, grab your journal, sit somewhere quiet or isolated, and write your thoughts down. What makes you feel out of alignment, overwhelmed, stressed, worried, annoyed, sad, or nervous.

2. Reflect about what happened, why you got nervous/sad/anxious, how you reacted at first, and list all the feelings that came to you at the moment.

Journaling Task 2

3. Can you find any limiting belief hidden in all the reasons you listed?

4. Could you have reacted in a different way? What ways?

5. What would be the positive aspects of having reacted differently to what happened?

6. Go back to the list of feelings you felt at the moment the situation happened. Go through each feeling and try to recall what were you thinking at the exact moment you felt that?

Journaling Task 2

7. Out of this list you made, separate two feelings that you want to feel less of during the week. For instance, let's say you want to feel less angry during this week.

- What actions can you take to feel less angry? How can you feel calmer when you are angry? Pick one action and commit to doing it next time anger comes in.

- Do this exact same exercise for the two feelings you chose and keep yourself accountable during the week. Every time you are about to feel that feeling, take the action that will make you feel a bit better.

Journaling Task 2

Day 4:
Date:

1, Every time that something happens and takes you away from your calm, count to 10, breathe deeply, grab your journal, sit somewhere quiet or isolated, and write your thoughts down. What makes you feel out of alignment, overwhelmed, stressed, worried, annoyed, sad, or nervous.

2. Reflect about what happened, why you got nervous/sad/anxious, how you reacted at first, and list all the feelings that came to you at the moment.

Journaling Task 2

3. Can you find any limiting belief hidden in all the reasons you listed?

4. Could you have reacted in a different way? What ways?

5. What would be the positive aspects of having reacted differently to what happened?

6. Go back to the list of feelings you felt at the moment the situation happened. Go through each feeling and try to recall what were you thinking at the exact moment you felt that?

Journaling Task 2

7. Out of this list you made, separate two feelings that you want to feel less of during the week. For instance, let's say you want to feel less angry during this week.

- What actions can you take to feel less angry? How can you feel calmer when you are angry? Pick one action and commit to doing it next time anger comes in.

- Do this exact same exercise for the two feelings you chose and keep yourself accountable during the week. Every time you are about to feel that feeling, take the action that will make you feel a bit better.

Journaling Task 2

Day 5:
Date:

1, Every time that something happens and takes you away from your calm, count to 10, breathe deeply, grab your journal, sit somewhere quiet or isolated, and write your thoughts down. What makes you feel out of alignment, overwhelmed, stressed, worried, annoyed, sad, or nervous.

2. Reflect about what happened, why you got nervous/sad/anxious, how you reacted at first, and list all the feelings that came to you at the moment.

Journaling Task 2

3. Can you find any limiting belief hidden in all the reasons you listed?

4. Could you have reacted in a different way? What ways?

5. What would be the positive aspects of having reacted differently to what happened?

6. Go back to the list of feelings you felt at the moment the situation happened. Go through each feeling and try to recall what were you thinking at the exact moment you felt that?

Journaling Task 2

7. Out of this list you made, separate two feelings that you want to feel less of during the week. For instance, let's say you want to feel less angry during this week.

- What actions can you take to feel less angry? How can you feel calmer when you are angry? Pick one action and commit to doing it next time anger comes in.

- Do this exact same exercise for the two feelings you chose and keep yourself accountable during the week. Every time you are about to feel that feeling, take the action that will make you feel a bit better.

Journaling Task 2

Day 6:
Date:

1, Every time that something happens and takes you away from your calm, count to 10, breathe deeply, grab your journal, sit somewhere quiet or isolated, and write your thoughts down. What makes you feel out of alignment, overwhelmed, stressed, worried, annoyed, sad, or nervous.

2. Reflect about what happened, why you got nervous/sad/anxious, how you reacted at first, and list all the feelings that came to you at the moment.

Journaling Task 2

3. Can you find any limiting belief hidden in all the reasons you listed?

4. Could you have reacted in a different way? What ways?

5. What would be the positive aspects of having reacted differently to what happened?

6. Go back to the list of feelings you felt at the moment the situation happened. Go through each feeling and try to recall what were you thinking at the exact moment you felt that?

Journaling Task 2

7. Out of this list you made, separate two feelings that you want to feel less of during the week. For instance, let's say you want to feel less angry during this week.

- What actions can you take to feel less angry? How can you feel calmer when you are angry? Pick one action and commit to doing it next time anger comes in.

- Do this exact same exercise for the two feelings you chose and keep yourself accountable during the week. Every time you are about to feel that feeling, take the action that will make you feel a bit better.

Journaling Task 2

Day 7:
Date:

1. Every time that something happens and takes you away from your calm, count to 10, breathe deeply, grab your journal, sit somewhere quiet or isolated, and write your thoughts down. What makes you feel out of alignment, overwhelmed, stressed, worried, annoyed, sad, or nervous.

2. Reflect about what happened, why you got nervous/sad/anxious, how you reacted at first, and list all the feelings that came to you at the moment.

Journaling Task 2

3. Can you find any limiting belief hidden in all the reasons you listed?

4. Could you have reacted in a different way? What ways?

5. What would be the positive aspects of having reacted differently to what happened?

6. Go back to the list of feelings you felt at the moment the situation happened. Go through each feeling and try to recall what were you thinking at the exact moment you felt that?

Journaling Task 2

7. Out of this list you made, separate two feelings that you want to feel less of during the week. For instance, let's say you want to feel less angry during this week.

    - What actions can you take to feel less angry? How can you feel calmer when you are angry? Pick one action and commit to doing it next time anger comes in.

    - Do this exact same exercise for the two feelings you chose and keep yourself accountable during the week. Every time you are about to feel that feeling, take the action that will make you feel a bit better.

Observing your emotions coming, catching yourself before they take you out of control, and redirecting your attitude to something that will make you feel a bit calmer is an excellent way of training your brain to look for a better feeling, and, at the same time, elevating your vibration.

This is not an exercise that you will do once and it will solve all your problems. You need to commit to long-term training and likely lifelong training. Unpredictable situations will always come our way, but we certainly have control over how we decide to react to what happens to us.

Affirmations For Vibrational Match

- The universe always has my back
- I am calm and peaceful
- I know that everything I want is coming to me
- I focus on the things I have total control in my life: My thoughts, my feelings, my attitudes, and my words
- I protect my energy above all. All is well and I am well
- I am a divine being and I radiate love everywhere I go
- I am bringing my deepest desires to my reality
- I trust the universe and the universe feels my positive energy
- I am a loving being and I surround myself with loving people
- I am already feeling my desires here with me. I am happy and excited for them
- I can and I will

The third and last step towards becoming a vibrational match is training yourself to really feel the excitement for all the manifestations that are already on their way.

For that, you will need to start practicing what is called **visualization** and bring yourself to a state of awe while imagining your desires already here with you.

There are a multitude of techniques to choose from, and you don't need to choose only one, you can practice all of them if that is what makes you feel good.

Visualization techniques are often paired with mindfulness meditation and guided meditations, but you are free to choose the practice that suits you better and aligns with your lifestyle as well.

Some of the visualization techniques we are covering here in the book are:
- Future self-journaling
- Manifesting your dream life guided meditation
- Abundance tracker journal
- Daily intention-setting
- Gratitude jar
- Manifesting with crystals

Let's start setting the mood by practicing a manifestation meditation so that you can set your manifestation intentions, get clear and specific about what you are bringing into your physical world, and bring yourself to a calm and peaceful state.

Remember: Guided meditations can be practiced either lying down or sitting in a traditional meditation pose like the lotus pose. Preferably, choose a quiet and isolated place/room where you won't be disturbed, prepare the ambiance to receive positive energies using what makes you feel cozy and relaxed: Soft cushions, a soft rug, scented candles, low lighting, fairy/string lights, your favorite aromas in the air (aromatherapy), healing crystals around the room and close to you, a vision board on the wall to make it easier for you to visualize what you want to manifest, or relaxing music playing to set the mood.

Of course, if you don't have all of these items available, prepare the room with what you have there and what makes you feel aligned with your manifestations.

- Position yourself comfortably and close your eyes. Align your neck with your spine and relax your whole body. Take a deep breath in and slowly another breath out. Repeat that three times.
- Keep your eyes closed and try to tune into your breath, paying attention to its rhythm. Feel yourself grounding. Focus on what you are feeling, release any tension from your body.
- Now, focus on the sensations that this room is giving you. Focus on the smells, the sounds, the texture of the things close to you or touching you.
- What can you feel from this room? What can you smell there? What do the smells remind you of? A place? People you love? A specific experience?

- Calmly take your mind into these sensations. Feel them deeply.
- Then, return to the present moment, to the here and now.
- Take another deep breath in and another long breath out.
- Envision yourself calmly floating to a different place and time. Imagine you are arriving at your magic place, that place you have always dreamed of.
- What can you see? Is it the beach? The mountains? Is it another city in another country? What is there in the place? What are you doing there? Feel the texture of where you are walking. Are you barefoot? Wearing heels? Casual shoes?
- Look everywhere around in this magical place of yours. Is there somebody else there with you? Who is it? What are they doing there? Are they celebrating something?
- What are you doing there? How are you dressed? How are you feeling?
- Then, slowly go toward a beautiful mirror you see right there close to you.
- Loom at the mirror. Who do you see?
- You slowly realize you are looking straight at your best self. Your higher self. The best version of you. How do you see yourself? What do you look like?
- Observe your posture, your movements, your happiness, and look yourself straight into your eyes. What do you feel?

- Feel the energy emanating from you and filling the whole space in. You are at your most magical place. You are your most perfect version. Who are you?
- Allow all this vitality and radiance to enter your whole heart and soul. Feel all this great energy and excitement in the bottom of your soul, let it spread around until there is no space for any other feeling to come in.
- Now, let this version of you become one with you. Feel it in your whole body, mind, and soul.
- Take a long, deep breath in and out. Slowly, come back to the here and now. Bring all that energy along with you. Absorb all that excitement and open your eyes.

How are you feeling now? Are you ready to receive all the good this universe has stored for you? Are you ready to start manifesting all those desires and bring them into your reality here and now?

Affirmations For Visualization

- I am a powerful manifestor
- I am love. I am receiving all the love in the universe
- I am capable
- I am open to all new experiences and opportunities coming my way
- I can and I will

Speaking Your Dreams Into Existence

───────⊸༻❀༺⊶───────

Within all of us is a divine capacity to manifest and attract all that we need and desire
- Wayne Dyer

That we are one with the universe you already know, right? So, it goes without saying that if you want to manifest anything meaningful in your life, you should pay attention to the many <u>signs</u> the universe sends you. When you speak your dreams into existence with all your heart, the universe, in turn, will keep sending you these signs, showing you the right path to be followed.

Do you recall any moment in which you had an urge, a strong feeling, or desire to take some action and follow a different path? Well, that was the universe speaking to you, sending you what we call an inspired action.

Inspired actions are without a doubt critical steps to be taken when it comes to the whole law of attraction process. It's all about doing something with a very strong emotion attached to it, and that surely will take you closer to your ultimate goal.

More often than not, you simply can't explain where that feeling came from, or why you suddenly started feeling drawn to it. However, that weird feeling is exactly the one that is directing you to the right path. You probably have already heard of that feeling with the name of intuition.

That's why it's so important to learn how to get in touch with your intuition and learn how to start paying attention to all the signs the universe sends you through it.
There is a quite common and big problem preventing most of us from understanding and noticing the universe's signs, though. Worry and anxiety.

Being a man or woman in this time, here and now, comes with a lot of anxiety and worries, partly because of our natural hormonal changes, but also because of the way our society is organized to all that "hustle and bustle" mentality. If you suffer from anxiety and excessive worry, you most likely have a hard time connecting to your soul and your intuition, and in turn, you barely notice the universe speaking to you.

Regulating your emotions and learning to bring yourself to calm again is an important step if you truly want to connect with the universe and with your higher self - to then start taking inspired actions and manifesting your dreams into reality.

Do you remember that famous law-of-attraction process: Ask, believe, receive?

That's it. You first speak your dreams into existence (ask), then you believe wholeheartedly that your desire is coming your way through putting out into the universe the right energy full of positive emotions, and finally you receive from the universe different signs and gut feelings directing you to your path so that you take inspired action to materialize your wishes and dreams into our physical world.

Have you noticed what is the commonality among all these steps?

The one element present in all of them is your emotions. Everything you think, say, and do must be filled with passion and enthusiasm so that the universe catches all that vibration and sends it back to you, materializing what you dream of.

Let's start on this manifestation process, then.

Speaking Your Dreams Into Existence - Techniques

Future Self Journaling

This law-of-attraction tool is oftentimes called scripting as well. It's a really powerful <u>technique</u> that involves a great deal of emotional output. It is also a really creative technique in which you have total freedom to use your whole imagination to create not only your future self but also your future reality.

The aim here is to focus all your attention and passion on the person you are becoming in this manifestation journey.

- What does your best self look like?
- How does he/she speak, act, and position him/herself in life?
- What is he/she like? What are his/her strongest characteristics and traits?
- What energy does he/she emanate?
- What kind of people does he/she surround him/herself with?
- What kind of activities does he/she engage in on a daily basis?
- What places does he/she go often?
- What does he/she do for a living?
- Where does he/she live?

Go through all of these questions and be really specific about every little detail. The universe can only deliver something to you when you are 100% sure of what you want.

Now that you already know who you are becoming, it's time to create your future reality by imagining yourself living a certain day exactly one year from today.

Because this is a **free-writing activity**, you can take the time you need to detail everything about this specific day in your future a year from now. Go to our reflection page below and write at the top of the page the date and hour you are imagining yourself in.

You can use the following questions as a guideline for your writing, but don't be too strict about it. Free yourself from limitations and just write everything that your heart longs for. You can describe how you are experiencing the day in question or you can write as if it has already happened - as if the day was already over. Start in the morning and go all the way to your afternoon, evening, and night.

Be as specific as possible and pour all your heart into everything you describe. Remember: Everything about your manifestations comes down to your emotions.

Sample questions;

- What day is it?
- How is the weather? The temperature?
- How would things be if this was your most perfect day?
- How would your day begin and how would it end?
- Who would you like to be with on your perfect day?
- How did your morning begin? What did you do first thing in the morning?
- How were you feeling? How was your energy that morning?
- What activities did you engage in? Were you alone? With friends or family?
- How was the overall mood that morning?
- What did you eat and drink? Where?
- Where did you go that day?
- What happened there?
- Did you enjoy the places you went?
- Where were you in the world? What city? Country?
- What was special about that day?
- How were you feeling during the whole day?
- What was your favorite part of the day? Why?
- What activities would you certainly repeat on another day?
- Did something unexpected happen? What?

Reflection Time
Future Self Journaling

Date:
Hour:

Reflection Time
Future Self Journaling

Date:

Hour:

Reflection Time
Future Self Journaling

Date:
Hour:

Reflection Time
Future Self Journaling

Date:
Hour:

Reflection Time
Future Self Journaling

Date:
Hour:

Reflection Time
Future Self Journaling

Date:
Hour:

Reflection Time
Future Self Journaling

Date:
Hour:

Reflection Time
Future Self Journaling

Date:

Hour:

Reflection Time
Future Self Journaling

Date:

Hour:

Reflection Time
Future Self Journaling

Date:
Hour:

Reflection Time
Future Self Journaling

Date:

Hour:

Reflection Time
Future Self Journaling

Date:

Hour:

Reflection Time
Future Self Journaling

Date:
Hour:

Reflection Time
Future Self Journaling

Date:

Hour:

Reflection Time
Future Self Journaling

Date:
Hour:

Reflection Time
Future Self Journaling

Date:
Hour:

Reflection Time
Future Self Journaling

Date:

Hour:

Reflection Time
Future Self Journaling

Date:

Hour:

Reflection Time
Future Self Journaling

Date:

Hour:

Reflection Time
Future Self Journaling

Date:
Hour:

Reflection Time
Future Self Journaling

Date:

Hour:

Reflection Time
Future Self Journaling

Date:

Hour:

Reflection Time
Future Self Journaling

Date:
Hour:

Reflection Time
Future Self Journaling

Date:
Hour:

Reflection Time
Future Self Journaling

Date:
Hour:

Reflection Time
Future Self Journaling

Date:

Hour:

Reflection Time
Future Self Journaling

Date:

Hour:

Reflection Time
Future Self Journaling

Date:

Hour:

Reflection Time
Future Self Journaling

Date:
Hour:

Reflection Time
Future Self Journaling

Date:

Hour:

Reflection Time
Future Self Journaling

Date:

Hour:

Gratitude Jar

What's the point of experiencing your deepest desires if you weren't grateful for them, right?

Gratitude is a key element in manifesting the life you dream of, and it's not just something you do when you receive something you want, but rather, it's more of a lifestyle you adopt and live by. Gratitude is also the basic component of happiness since there is no way someone can be grateful and sad simultaneously.

This activity works as a constant reminder that there's always something good going on in our lives. All we need to do is pause, breath in deeply, and intentionally look for these good moments happening around us. It's a way of training our minds not to get swept away by the negatives but to be in awe and notice all the magic hidden in the little joys of our everyday life.

For this activity, all you need is a glass jar, a couple of colorful post-its, and your favorite glitter/colorful pens.

- Choose the frequency you will practice this activity - it can either be every day/every other day/or twice a week - do it as you please.
- During these specific days, choose a time of day to sit quietly and recall all the moments in which you had a reason to smile, recall something that made you feel happy on that day, or even a nice surprise you had.
- Write each moment separately on a different post-it. Fold it and put it into the jar.
- Keep your jar somewhere visible and in easy access so that you don't get caught in all the business of the day and forget about it.
- Repeat the same process on all those chosen days.
- Select a specific day of the week/month as your sacred day - just like a ritual - to open your jar and go through all your beautiful and happy moments. You can even take advantage of the situation and gather your loved ones so that you all recall and cherish these moments together.

This is a really beautiful activity that inspires joy and makes you realize all the good things to be grateful for in your life.

We are going to dedicate a whole chapter ahead to discuss the benefits of gratitude in our lives and how you can incorporate more of it into your everyday routine.

Intention-Setting

Law of attraction is all about intentions. They are the backbone of all the power you put out into the world. Your manifestation is the physical form of what you want to bring into this world, and intentions are what carries all the emotional force that will direct your energy to what you want. It goes without saying that if they are the emotional force, you don't have to use them solely to manifest situations and events but to manifest how you want to feel and how you want to show up on that specific day. Intentions can be set by simply putting a lot of emotion into what you are visualizing, or going through a more in-depth practice like scripting or the gratitude jar. Intentions not only shape the reality you are creating but also set the mood you live in.

You can either choose to set intentions daily, weekly, monthly, yearly, during the full moon, new moon, or even on New Year's Eve.

How does setting intentions work?

Reflection Time
Intention-Setting

Setting the Mood

This is the time to connect with your soul and to create a cozy and relaxing atmosphere around you. Light your favorite scented candle, decorate the room with your favorite objects, burn some sage if you prefer, or organize your favorite crystals around to cleanse the energy and bring more positivity in.

Getting Aligned and Meditating

Now it's the time to really get inspired and play with your imagination.
Choose a mantra or an anchoring theme to stick to during the whole ritual. Make them coherent to your focal intentions. You can even use some tarot/oracle deck cards to guide you. The most important thing here is to tune into your intuition and let it be your guide.

Journaling Your Intentions

Like I said - let your imagination flow here. Describe how you want to feel today/this week/this month. Describe what you want to happen in your life during this period, who you want to meet, where you want to go. During the whole writing process, describe how you feel using strong emotional words like excited, magical, unforgettable, memorable, etc.

Reflection Time
Intention-Setting

Speaking Your Intentions Out to the Universe

This is a moment to express yourself and show the universe you are really excited, even at the thought that your intentions are being manifested. Just be yourself here and read your script out loud showing you are truly happy for everything you are about to bring into reality. If you are a more extroverted woman, you can even set some music that inspires you and dance your intentions out. If you play the guitar, rehearse some pieces to make you get into alignment. If you are a more introverted person, grab your favorite hot beverage, sit quietly, and meditate on your intentions. You do you. Do it as you please.

Revisit Your Intentions Often

Get into the habit of going back and reading through your notes from time to time so that you bring yourself into alignment, whenever you feel it's necessary.

Abundance Tracker

A truth everyone needs to realize is that everything you want to experience will be a direct result of the way you show up in this world, your state of mind, and a result of the energy you put out into the world. Do you want more abundance in your life? So, <u>feel</u> the abundance around you.

Something that not everyone realizes is that we don't create abundance. What we end up creating are limitations, simply because abundance itself is already everywhere.

The world is an abundant place. Nature is abundant of beauty, magic, and a variety of beings everywhere you look; life is abundant of experiences, synchronicities, people coming into your life, and especially abundant of feelings and emotions. The universe is abundant of mystery, of the unexplainable phenomena, abundant of planets, stars, and molecules. Abundance is undeniably everywhere. Human beings are the only ones creating their own limitations.

If you truly want to manifest more wealth and abundance in your life, you have to connect yourself with all the existing abundance around you and in the world.

How can you do that?

Create your own abundance tracker and deliberately train your mind to notice abundance around.

Important to note that the word abundance doesn't refer only to money and wealth. Money is something man-made and, in reality, money is pure energy. Abundance is the natural state of the universe. If you intentionally pause to notice it, you will realize that shifting your perspective allows you to start seeing it everywhere.

- Have you ever paid attention to the abundance of people living on our planet? Over 7,753 billion.
- Have you ever noticed the abundance of food produced to feed all of them?
- Have you ever noticed how abundant planet Earth is just by offering us everything we need to live for almost 100 years on it?
- Have you ever noticed the abundance of existing cities/countries?
- Have you ever noticed the abundance of creativity going on so that every little product you use could have been made?
- Have you ever noticed the abundance of complaints on the internet nowadays?
- Have you ever noticed the abundance of buildings being designed/projected/ and executed around the world?
- Have you ever noticed the abundance of people going out and having fun?
- Have you ever noticed the abundance of people who receive/don't receive love?
- Have you ever noticed the abundance of people going to work every day?

Whether you noticed it or not - abundance is always there. Even when you refer to lack. There is an abundance of lack as well. It's all about perspective.

To create your own abundance tracker, you will use the chart below for the **next two weeks** and will intentionally pay attention to everything that happens in your day during these two weeks.

You will train your mind for a whole week to be alert and in search for every sign of abundance around you. Carry this journal with you in the upcoming weeks and if you notice anything you consider abundance - take note of it.

At the end of every week, you will revisit your notes and go through your examples one by one and acknowledge the abundance in your life.

Reflection Time
Abundance Tracker

Monday

Tuesday

Wednesday

Thursday

Friday

Reflection Time
Abundance Tracker

Monday

Tuesday

Wednesday

Thursday

Friday

Affirmations For Abundance

- Abundance is everywhere in the universe
- I am one with the universe so abundance is part of who I am
- I am open to receiving wealth, health, and joy
- I am abundant
- I am capable of making more and more money every month
- I am a magnet attracting abundance into my life
- I have infinite potential. I am creative. I am wise. I am intelligent. I am enough
- I am capable of creating my own reality
- My reality is abundant
- I can and I will

Align Your Energy With What You Want From Life

One of the universal laws I didn't mention in my list at the beginning of the book is the <u>Law of Vibration</u>. This law's principle says that everything in our universe is always vibrating in constant circular movements, and that's why the energy you give out always returns to you.

This same energy you emanate and receive back indicates your vibrational frequency and determines the way you approach life.

This is the reason why when we mention vibrational frequency, we mean feelings and emotions. They are the ones that carry immense energy and power to attract what you want into your life. You always have to align your thoughts and your feelings so that manifestation really happens. Vibrational alignment is not magic at all, it's a choice you intentionally make every single day.

Let's be really clear here. I am not saying that you have to deny or suppress your negative emotions whatsoever. In fact, as I already stated in the other chapters, you have to feel all your feelings, negative and positive, but what you can't allow yourself to do is dwell on the negative ones. You cannot let yourself be consumed by them. Feel whatever you are feeling at the moment, embrace them and try to understand where they come from and why you were triggered, listen to the message your emotions are sending you, sit with them, and reflect on them.

Use your negative emotions to grow stronger and wiser, learn from them and then let them go, and finally learn how to bring yourself back to a calm state so that you allow the positive energy to guide you throughout your journey.

The more you practice this whole emotion regulation process, the higher your positive energy will be, and the faster you will align yourself with your deepest wishes.

Have you ever heard of The Emotional Guidance Scale created by authors Esther and Jerry Hicks? In their scale, they present the energetic frequencies of most of our human emotions. The highest frequencies come from feelings like joy, appreciation, freedom, empowerment, love, passion, happiness, and enthusiasm (pg. 114).

The more you train yourself to live a life guided by these feelings, the more aligned you will be, the easier your manifestations will come.

One of the most effective ways of bringing yourself back to calm is by practicing mindfulness meditation or guided meditations. Whenever you start feeling overwhelmed and anxious, pause, breathe in deeply, give a long and deep breath out, sit comfortably somewhere quiet, and let yourself sink into calmness.

Guided Meditation: Manifesting Your Dream Life

What do you aspire to achieve? Focus on one of your greatest dreams, something that means the world to you, and that you would be eternally grateful to the universe if it delivers it to you now.

- Sit comfortably on your mat or whatever you feel like. Go to lotus pose and rest both your hands palms up on your knees. Give a deep and long breath in and then out. Feel yourself grounding and relax your whole body and mind. Deep inhale and exhale again.
- Let go of any tension in your body, relax your shoulders, arms, relax your face, your mouth. Focus on a deep inhale and let it all out in a long exhale.
- Now, focus all your attention on the mantra you are affirming during all meditation, whenever you feel like.
- I am aligned with all the abundance, happiness, and prosperity in the world.
- Start feeling what abundance, happiness, and prosperity mean to you. Fill all your heart with excitement for receiving all the abundance and happiness you want from life.
- Bring to your mind everything that inspires happiness within you. Give another deep and long breath in and another one out. Breathe in all the happiness and prosperity and breathe out all the self-doubt and worries. Let them go. Stay with abundance, happiness, and prosperity within you.
- Visualize what you want to bring into your reality with all your heart.
- Repeat the mantra: <u>I am aligned with all abundance, happiness, and prosperity in the world</u>. Feel these words in your soul, in your heart. Believe in them.
- Focus on bringing all these feelings into your life now and start living by them.

- What is your most precious desire? What is your dearest dream? Imagine it. Feel it now. It's real and it's here now.
- Feel yourself living your dream. You are your dream. Your dream is you.
- Give another deep and long deep breath in and another one out.
- Repeat: <u>I am aligned with all the abundance, happiness, and prosperity in the world</u>.
- Now, slowly come back to the here and now. Breathe in and out deeply and open your eyes.
- Repeat: <u>I can and I will</u>.

How to Properly Use Positive Affirmations

Have you ever wondered what is the mind trick behind positive affirmations? They are not mere sentences you keep repeating in vain, but rather, they are powerful statements you repeat often so that you can train your brain to form a new belief system.

Whether or not you are conscious about it, you and everybody else in the world have always used affirmations to create negative and false beliefs about yourself. Isn't it odd that everyone repeats belittling statements about themselves on a daily basis for years without ever questioning the truth of it?

Recall those days when you keep repeating the same mistakes and without even thinking much you go and say I am such an idiot? Or maybe that skill you have been trying to learn with no success, and suddenly you lose your patience and keep repeating to yourself I will never learn that! I am such a dummy. Other times you may say I simply can't understand that! I always do everything wrong.

Do you know what happens when we all keep repeating such sentences during our whole lives? Yes. That's right. Your mind believes blindly in those affirmations and that's how your disempowering beliefs about yourself were born.

Our brain is wired to always look around for confirmation of what we believe to be true. So, why not start to form a new belief system about yourself? One that is more empowering, positive, bold, and uplifting? If you keep repeating it enough, your mind will believe it.

Affirmations For Positivity

- I am energy
- I am love. I radiate good feelings
- I am flowing with love and light.
- I choose to feel good. I am motivated by joy
- I know today is going to be a wonderful day
- I am open to new and wonderful things
- I am unlimited. I am full of joy
- I create a wonderful life for myself
- I am excited for the day today
- Life is good. I am grateful for every moment I am alive

The Power of Affirmations and Guided Meditations

Our subconscious mind is responsible for creating 95% of our reality, it's a part of our brain that is totally programmed and stores all of our old fears, ingrained beliefs, and memories. Our beliefs and fears were once experiences in which we attached so many emotions that they are constantly affecting our present reality.
Have you ever noticed that most of your decisions are based on previous experiences and on how you felt at the time they happened?

That's precisely why positive affirmations work. When we constantly repeat the same affirmations and are able to attach enough emotions to them, they are being slowly stored in our subconscious mind, and in turn, we end up reprogramming our minds.

The best way to attach emotions while repeating your affirmations is by pairing them with a guided meditation with some relaxing, calming music. Music containing subliminal or binaural beats has the power to access our subconscious mind through a meditative state. The subconscious mind is much more susceptible to auto-suggestion right before we fall asleep or right after waking up, that's why most meditation teachers tell you to meditate during these periods, but in reality, you can meditate whenever you want.

When using affirmations always select those ones that are aligned with what you are trying to manifest or with the feelings and emotions you want to bring more of into your life.

Affirmations for Self-Love

- Today I choose to be gentle with myself
- I can be, and I am my biggest supporter
- I believe in myself and in my inner power
- I trust myself to make decisions aligned with my soul and my heart
- I AM ENOUGH
- I have the power to change my life whenever I need
- I focus only on what I can control and I let go of what I can't
- My life is full of opportunities and I am open to the new
- I am strong and brave and I live my life to the fullest
- I am aware of my own desires, wishes, and needs and I honor them
- It's safe for me to be myself

Affirmations for Self-Love

- I express myself freely. I am always authentic and spontaneous
- I choose to feel good
- I choose to create the life I have always wanted for myself
- I always listen to my intuition
- I am aligned with my highest good
- I am in control of my own happiness
- I am really proud of how far I have come and I love the whole of me
- I embody love, kindness, and purpose
- I am open to all joy, love, happiness, and abundance in the world

Gratitude Is a Lifestyle

The more you feel good for what you currently have, the more you will attract to you.

So, many of us confuse being grateful with being complacent or even with accepting less than what we actually deserve from life.

It's totally possible to feel grateful for what you currently have AND strive for making things in your life better, for upgrading your lifestyle, and for growing as a person.

What is not possible whatsoever is saying you feel grateful but living life with a victim mentality, always focusing on the negative things happening in the world and blaming others for what you couldn't achieve, have, or do.

There is no way to be grateful and resentful at the same time. You have to choose which one you will live by.

Being grateful is much more than just saying thank you to everyone. It's a lifestyle in which you are truly connected with the little joys of life, with everything that makes you happy and fulfilled.

You don't take things for granted, you cherish, care, and express your love and gratitude whenever possible.

Gratitude is the key element to a happy life. Feeling genuinely grateful is a powerful way to shift your vibration from a low frequency to a higher one, and being such, it's also a <u>key element to call abundance into your life</u>.

So, how can you integrate more of it into your life?

One of the first attitudes to start feeling grateful is to ban complaints from your life. Just stop complaining and start appreciating instead. When we complain, we are tuned in to the negatives in life, and you don't want that, right?

What you want is to manifest your dream life into your reality, so you need to align yourself with feelings of gratitude, joy, happiness, and enthusiasm.

I already showed you how to create a gratitude jar to bring more of it into your life, now we are going to go through a more creative tool that is also a way of keeping you inspired through your manifestation journey.

Everyone who is interested in the law of attraction and personal development knows about the power of vision boards when it comes to manifesting our dreams, but what about creating a gratitude wall to practice gratitude as a constant ritual in your life?

Gratitude Wall

It works pretty much like a vision board, but instead of pinning your dreams and aspirations on a wall, you are going to reflect back on your life and get creative looking for everything that reminds you of something you are really grateful for.

These things don't need to only be photos, but also any object that reminds you of something valuable and important to you. The most important aspect of all this activity is making sure that everything that you stick to your gratitude wall really makes you smile while staring at them.

What you pin on the wall must inspire in your feelings of happiness, love, and gratitude. They can be things like personal photos, notes, cards, Pinterest pictures, magazine pictures, newspaper articles, reports, you name it. Your imagination is the limit.

Hang it on a wall you have easy access to and look at it as often as you please. The more, the merrier.

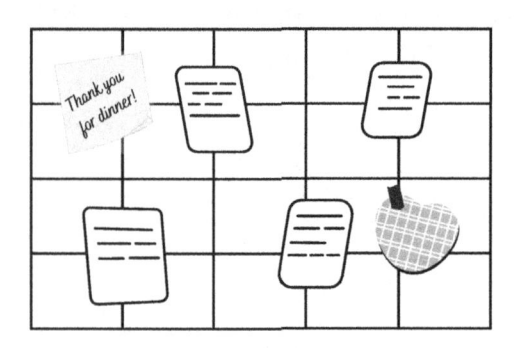

Affirmations For Gratitude

- I am grateful for whom I am becoming
- I am grateful for all that happened in my life for that I am who I am today
- I accept all the goodness in the world
- Everything flows easily into my life
- I am aligned with feelings of joy, happiness, and I am so grateful for being alive
- I love myself and I am grateful for the person I am today
- I love my life and I know that the universe has my back
- I am so grateful for all the experiences and opportunities that life has given me
- I am aware of my power to create my reality and I thank you universe for all the good energy I feel
- I feel so grateful for being loved and for loving
- My life is full of love and I am grateful for every person in it
- I fill my life with gratitude, joy, and happiness every single day
- I love my life and I love being me

Set Yourself Up to a Happier, Wealthier, and Fulfilling life

Whatever you want to create, believe it first in your mind, and then create it in your reality.

Whatever reality you have been experiencing, know that you have within you the power to change it. The only thing you need now is to start believing with all your heart that you really can change your life and transform it into one of love, abundance, and happiness.

Does that mean you won't experience sadness anymore? Of course, not.

Law of polarity. There will always be duality in the universe. To experience daylight, we have to go through the nighttime. To appreciate the moon, we need the sun to come out. Seasons come and go. There are those hot days, and then the freezing ones. There will always be love and hate on planet Earth as long as we humans live, because they are human feelings and we are human beings.

Remember: The only constant thing in our human existence is impermanence itself. Everything changes, and that is proof enough that the life you are living today is temporary. You can create a new life, a new you. It's a bold decision, but it's a decision only you can make. So, what are you deciding? Let's manifest your deepest desires and put your life into motion.

Affirmations to Create Your Reality

- The universe is a magical and powerful place
- I am one with the universe, so I am a powerful and magical being as well
- I can create a life I love and cherish
- I start creating the life I have always wanted right now
- My thoughts, feelings, and words I speak are all aligned with my most precious desires and dreams
- My good feelings attract all the good energy in the world
- Everything that I love flows easily to me
- I am always attracting abundance into my life
- I am one with the universe and I know that the universe always has my back
- I am aligned with the energy of money and abundance. Money flows easily into my life
- I see abundance everywhere I go

Affirmations to Create Your Reality

- I see love everywhere I go
- I see the good in everyone
- I intentionally and consciously choose to feel happy today
- I am calm and I always trust my intuition
- My intuition always shows me the right way to go
- I am energy and I am aligned
- The universe always sends everything I need to me
- I am a loving being and I spread love everywhere I go
- I am a powerful manifestor and I am always aligned with all the good in this universe.
- I am changing my reality into one of joy, love, happiness, and great abundance
- I can, and I will

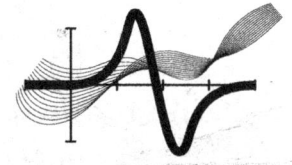

Manifest Your Happier Version

Being happy is not about having more, but rather, about choosing what you want to feel.
Only you can know what happiness truly means to you.
You are the only soul living in your body and in your mind, so no one can determine what makes you feel truly happy.

Always begin your day, week, month, and year asking yourself:

- What could I do today that would make me feel genuinely happy and content?
- How can I show myself some love today?
- In what ways did I love myself today?
- Who did I make happy today?
- Who brings me feelings of joy and happiness?
- Who do I truly love?
- What is the smallest step I can take today that will take me a bit closer to my greatest dream?

When you unapologetically decide to take action to start creating the life you truly deserve and want for yourself, the universe has no other way but to conspire in your favor, moving people, situations, and events all the way straight into your life.

One of the most efficient and famous law-of-attraction tools to manifest your desires is called scripting.

Scripting is a form of journaling that is focused on creating a new reality for your life.

When you start writing, you intentionally write about and script life exactly the way you want it to be. It's your future self pictured on paper. It's your most wanted outcome coming into your reality.

When scripting your new reality focus on the following questions as a reference on what to write about.

- What do I want my reality to be like?
- Where will I be living?
- Who will be the people I surround myself with?
- What will I be doing in this new reality?
- Whom will I be? What will be my strongest traits?
- How will I position myself in this world?
- What will be my purpose in life? Is it the same one I have today?
- Why do I want to create a new reality? What's wrong with this one I am living in now?
- What dreams will I be experiencing?
- What's better about me in this new reality?

Before going straight into scripting your new reality itself, it's crucial to show appreciation for what you already have in your life now that makes you feel good, content, and fulfilled. As we discussed previously, gratitude is a decisive element when manifesting your dream life.

So, take a moment and think through every detail in your current life that is working well and that you love. Write about it, reflect on these points, and thank the universe for all of it.

To create much more powerful energy, you should always script either in the present tense as if you were living that reality now, or in the past tense as if it had already happened and you were bringing the memories to paper. Be as specific as possible when writing your new reality. The more precise you are, the clearer your message to the universe is.

Always write/script feelings and show deep excitement for what is happening. When you write your emotions on paper, you are already shifting your whole energetic frequency and sending the universe the exact energy you want back to you.

Always write focusing on what you want to manifest and not on what you don't want.
Remember that we live in an attraction-based universe and the thoughts you think, the feelings you feel, and the words you speak determine the energetic frequency you are in.

You will always attract more of what you are sending the universe.

To start your scripting practice, you need to be connected with <u>good</u> energies, so never script if you are feeling sad, stressed, or overwhelmed. In such situations, first, work on your emotions and bring yourself back to a calm state, and then, practice whatever law of attraction technique you feel drawn to.

So manifestor, I guided you throughout this whole manifestation process so that you have in your hands the tools necessary to start your own journey towards the life you have always dreamed of.

Now, it's your turn to make a decision.

What are you manifesting and whom are you becoming in the process?

Thank you for allowing me to share this
Daily Manifestation Journal Book with you.
Special thanks for leaving a review on Amazon.

*I wish upon you happiness, love, and abundance
in all of your future endeavors.*

Reflection Time
Scripting My New Reality

Date:

- What could I do today that would make me feel genuinely happy and content?

- How can I show myself some love today?

- In what ways did I love myself today?

- Who did I make happy today?

- Who brings me feelings of joy and happiness?

- Who do I truly love?

- What is the smallest step I can take today that will take me a bit closer to my greatest dream?

Reflection Time
Scripting My New Reality

Date:

- What could I do today that would make me feel genuinely happy and content?

- How can I show myself some love today?

- In what ways did I love myself today?

- Who did I make happy today?

- Who brings me feelings of joy and happiness?

- Who do I truly love?

- What is the smallest step I can take today that will take me a bit closer to my greatest dream?

Reflection Time
Scripting My New Reality

Date:

- What could I do today that would make me feel genuinely happy and content?

- How can I show myself some love today?

- In what ways did I love myself today?

- Who did I make happy today?

- Who brings me feelings of joy and happiness?

- Who do I truly love?

- What is the smallest step I can take today that will take me a bit closer to my greatest dream?

Reflection Time
Scripting My New Reality

Date:

- What could I do today that would make me feel genuinely happy and content?

- How can I show myself some love today?

- In what ways did I love myself today?

- Who did I make happy today?

- Who brings me feelings of joy and happiness?

- Who do I truly love?

- What is the smallest step I can take today that will take me a bit closer to my greatest dream?

Reflection Time
Scripting My New Reality

Date:

- What could I do today that would make me feel genuinely happy and content?

- How can I show myself some love today?

- In what ways did I love myself today?

- Who did I make happy today?

- Who brings me feelings of joy and happiness?

- Who do I truly love?

- What is the smallest step I can take today that will take me a bit closer to my greatest dream?

Reflection Time
Scripting My New Reality

Date:

- What could I do today that would make me feel genuinely happy and content?

- How can I show myself some love today?

- In what ways did I love myself today?

- Who did I make happy today?

- Who brings me feelings of joy and happiness?

- Who do I truly love?

- What is the smallest step I can take today that will take me a bit closer to my greatest dream?

Reflection Time
Scripting My New Reality

Date:

- What could I do today that would make me feel genuinely happy and content?

- How can I show myself some love today?

- In what ways did I love myself today?

- Who did I make happy today?

- Who brings me feelings of joy and happiness?

- Who do I truly love?

- What is the smallest step I can take today that will take me a bit closer to my greatest dream?

Reflection Time
Scripting My New Reality

Date:

- What could I do today that would make me feel genuinely happy and content?

- How can I show myself some love today?

- In what ways did I love myself today?

- Who did I make happy today?

- Who brings me feelings of joy and happiness?

- Who do I truly love?

- What is the smallest step I can take today that will take me a bit closer to my greatest dream?

Reflection Time
Scripting My New Reality

Date:

- What could I do today that would make me feel genuinely happy and content?

- How can I show myself some love today?

- In what ways did I love myself today?

- Who did I make happy today?

- Who brings me feelings of joy and happiness?

- Who do I truly love?

- What is the smallest step I can take today that will take me a bit closer to my greatest dream?

Reflection Time
Scripting My New Reality

Date:

- What could I do today that would make me feel genuinely happy and content?

- How can I show myself some love today?

- In what ways did I love myself today?

- Who did I make happy today?

- Who brings me feelings of joy and happiness?

- Who do I truly love?

- What is the smallest step I can take today that will take me a bit closer to my greatest dream?

Reflection Time
Scripting My New Reality

Date:

- What could I do today that would make me feel genuinely happy and content?

- How can I show myself some love today?

- In what ways did I love myself today?

- Who did I make happy today?

- Who brings me feelings of joy and happiness?

- Who do I truly love?

- What is the smallest step I can take today that will take me a bit closer to my greatest dream?

Reflection Time
Scripting My New Reality

Date:

- What could I do today that would make me feel genuinely happy and content?

- How can I show myself some love today?

- In what ways did I love myself today?

- Who did I make happy today?

- Who brings me feelings of joy and happiness?

- Who do I truly love?

- What is the smallest step I can take today that will take me a bit closer to my greatest dream?

Reflection Time
Scripting My New Reality

Date:

- What could I do today that would make me feel genuinely happy and content?

- How can I show myself some love today?

- In what ways did I love myself today?

- Who did I make happy today?

- Who brings me feelings of joy and happiness?

- Who do I truly love?

- What is the smallest step I can take today that will take me a bit closer to my greatest dream?

Reflection Time
Scripting My New Reality

Date:

- What could I do today that would make me feel genuinely happy and content?

- How can I show myself some love today?

- In what ways did I love myself today?

- Who did I make happy today?

- Who brings me feelings of joy and happiness?

- Who do I truly love?

- What is the smallest step I can take today that will take me a bit closer to my greatest dream?

Reflection Time
Scripting My New Reality

Date:

- What could I do today that would make me feel genuinely happy and content?

- How can I show myself some love today?

- In what ways did I love myself today?

- Who did I make happy today?

- Who brings me feelings of joy and happiness?

- Who do I truly love?

- What is the smallest step I can take today that will take me a bit closer to my greatest dream?

Reflection Time
Scripting My New Reality

Date:

- What could I do today that would make me feel genuinely happy and content?

- How can I show myself some love today?

- In what ways did I love myself today?

- Who did I make happy today?

- Who brings me feelings of joy and happiness?

- Who do I truly love?

- What is the smallest step I can take today that will take me a bit closer to my greatest dream?

Reflection Time
Scripting My New Reality

Date:

- What could I do today that would make me feel genuinely happy and content?

- How can I show myself some love today?

- In what ways did I love myself today?

- Who did I make happy today?

- Who brings me feelings of joy and happiness?

- Who do I truly love?

- What is the smallest step I can take today that will take me a bit closer to my greatest dream?

Reflection Time
Scripting My New Reality

Date:

- What could I do today that would make me feel genuinely happy and content?

- How can I show myself some love today?

- In what ways did I love myself today?

- Who did I make happy today?

- Who brings me feelings of joy and happiness?

- Who do I truly love?

- What is the smallest step I can take today that will take me a bit closer to my greatest dream?

Reflection Time
Scripting My New Reality

Date:

- What could I do today that would make me feel genuinely happy and content?

- How can I show myself some love today?

- In what ways did I love myself today?

- Who did I make happy today?

- Who brings me feelings of joy and happiness?

- Who do I truly love?

- What is the smallest step I can take today that will take me a bit closer to my greatest dream?

Reflection Time
Scripting My New Reality

Date:

- What could I do today that would make me feel genuinely happy and content?

- How can I show myself some love today?

- In what ways did I love myself today?

- Who did I make happy today?

- Who brings me feelings of joy and happiness?

- Who do I truly love?

- What is the smallest step I can take today that will take me a bit closer to my greatest dream?

Reflection Time
Scripting My New Reality

Date:

- What could I do today that would make me feel genuinely happy and content?

- How can I show myself some love today?

- In what ways did I love myself today?

- Who did I make happy today?

- Who brings me feelings of joy and happiness?

- Who do I truly love?

- What is the smallest step I can take today that will take me a bit closer to my greatest dream?

Reflection Time
Scripting My New Reality

Date:

- What could I do today that would make me feel genuinely happy and content?

- How can I show myself some love today?

- In what ways did I love myself today?

- Who did I make happy today?

- Who brings me feelings of joy and happiness?

- Who do I truly love?

- What is the smallest step I can take today that will take me a bit closer to my greatest dream?

Reflection Time
Scripting My New Reality

Date:

- What could I do today that would make me feel genuinely happy and content?

- How can I show myself some love today?

- In what ways did I love myself today?

- Who did I make happy today?

- Who brings me feelings of joy and happiness?

- Who do I truly love?

- What is the smallest step I can take today that will take me a bit closer to my greatest dream?

Reflection Time
Scripting My New Reality

Date:

- What could I do today that would make me feel genuinely happy and content?

- How can I show myself some love today?

- In what ways did I love myself today?

- Who did I make happy today?

- Who brings me feelings of joy and happiness?

- Who do I truly love?

- What is the smallest step I can take today that will take me a bit closer to my greatest dream?

Reflection Time
Scripting My New Reality

Date:

- What could I do today that would make me feel genuinely happy and content?

- How can I show myself some love today?

- In what ways did I love myself today?

- Who did I make happy today?

- Who brings me feelings of joy and happiness?

- Who do I truly love?

- What is the smallest step I can take today that will take me a bit closer to my greatest dream?

Reflection Time
Scripting My New Reality

Date:

- What could I do today that would make me feel genuinely happy and content?

- How can I show myself some love today?

- In what ways did I love myself today?

- Who did I make happy today?

- Who brings me feelings of joy and happiness?

- Who do I truly love?

- What is the smallest step I can take today that will take me a bit closer to my greatest dream?

Reflection Time
Scripting My New Reality

Date:

- What could I do today that would make me feel genuinely happy and content?

- How can I show myself some love today?

- In what ways did I love myself today?

- Who did I make happy today?

- Who brings me feelings of joy and happiness?

- Who do I truly love?

- What is the smallest step I can take today that will take me a bit closer to my greatest dream?

Reflection Time
Scripting My New Reality

Date:

- What could I do today that would make me feel genuinely happy and content?

- How can I show myself some love today?

- In what ways did I love myself today?

- Who did I make happy today?

- Who brings me feelings of joy and happiness?

- Who do I truly love?

- What is the smallest step I can take today that will take me a bit closer to my greatest dream?

Reflection Time
Scripting My New Reality

Date:

- What could I do today that would make me feel genuinely happy and content?

- How can I show myself some love today?

- In what ways did I love myself today?

- Who did I make happy today?

- Who brings me feelings of joy and happiness?

- Who do I truly love?

- What is the smallest step I can take today that will take me a bit closer to my greatest dream?

Reflection Time
Scripting My New Reality

Date:

- What could I do today that would make me feel genuinely happy and content?

- How can I show myself some love today?

- In what ways did I love myself today?

- Who did I make happy today?

- Who brings me feelings of joy and happiness?

- Who do I truly love?

- What is the smallest step I can take today that will take me a bit closer to my greatest dream?

Reflection Time
Scripting My New Reality

Date:

- What could I do today that would make me feel genuinely happy and content?

- How can I show myself some love today?

- In what ways did I love myself today?

- Who did I make happy today?

- Who brings me feelings of joy and happiness?

- Who do I truly love?

- What is the smallest step I can take today that will take me a bit closer to my greatest dream?

Reflection Time
Scripting My New Reality

Date:

- What could I do today that would make me feel genuinely happy and content?

- How can I show myself some love today?

- In what ways did I love myself today?

- Who did I make happy today?

- Who brings me feelings of joy and happiness?

- Who do I truly love?

- What is the smallest step I can take today that will take me a bit closer to my greatest dream?

Reflection Time
Scripting My New Reality

Date:

- What could I do today that would make me feel genuinely happy and content?

- How can I show myself some love today?

- In what ways did I love myself today?

- Who did I make happy today?

- Who brings me feelings of joy and happiness?

- Who do I truly love?

- What is the smallest step I can take today that will take me a bit closer to my greatest dream?

Reflection Time
Scripting My New Reality

Date:

- What could I do today that would make me feel genuinely happy and content?

- How can I show myself some love today?

- In what ways did I love myself today?

- Who did I make happy today?

- Who brings me feelings of joy and happiness?

- Who do I truly love?

- What is the smallest step I can take today that will take me a bit closer to my greatest dream?

Reflection Time
Scripting My New Reality

Date:

- What could I do today that would make me feel genuinely happy and content?

- How can I show myself some love today?

- In what ways did I love myself today?

- Who did I make happy today?

- Who brings me feelings of joy and happiness?

- Who do I truly love?

- What is the smallest step I can take today that will take me a bit closer to my greatest dream?

Reflection Time
Scripting My New Reality

Date:

- What could I do today that would make me feel genuinely happy and content?

- How can I show myself some love today?

- In what ways did I love myself today?

- Who did I make happy today?

- Who brings me feelings of joy and happiness?

- Who do I truly love?

- What is the smallest step I can take today that will take me a bit closer to my greatest dream?

Reflection Time
Scripting My New Reality

Date:

- What could I do today that would make me feel genuinely happy and content?

- How can I show myself some love today?

- In what ways did I love myself today?

- Who did I make happy today?

- Who brings me feelings of joy and happiness?

- Who do I truly love?

- What is the smallest step I can take today that will take me a bit closer to my greatest dream?

Reflection Time
Scripting My New Reality

Date:

- What could I do today that would make me feel genuinely happy and content?

- How can I show myself some love today?

- In what ways did I love myself today?

- Who did I make happy today?

- Who brings me feelings of joy and happiness?

- Who do I truly love?

- What is the smallest step I can take today that will take me a bit closer to my greatest dream?

Reflection Time
Scripting My New Reality

Date:

- What could I do today that would make me feel genuinely happy and content?

- How can I show myself some love today?

- In what ways did I love myself today?

- Who did I make happy today?

- Who brings me feelings of joy and happiness?

- Who do I truly love?

- What is the smallest step I can take today that will take me a bit closer to my greatest dream?

Reflection Time
Scripting My New Reality

Date:

- What could I do today that would make me feel genuinely happy and content?

- How can I show myself some love today?

- In what ways did I love myself today?

- Who did I make happy today?

- Who brings me feelings of joy and happiness?

- Who do I truly love?

- What is the smallest step I can take today that will take me a bit closer to my greatest dream?

Reflection Time
Scripting My New Reality

Date:

- What could I do today that would make me feel genuinely happy and content?

- How can I show myself some love today?

- In what ways did I love myself today?

- Who did I make happy today?

- Who brings me feelings of joy and happiness?

- Who do I truly love?

- What is the smallest step I can take today that will take me a bit closer to my greatest dream?

Reflection Time
Scripting My New Reality

Date:

- What could I do today that would make me feel genuinely happy and content?

- How can I show myself some love today?

- In what ways did I love myself today?

- Who did I make happy today?

- Who brings me feelings of joy and happiness?

- Who do I truly love?

- What is the smallest step I can take today that will take me a bit closer to my greatest dream?

Reflection Time
Scripting My New Reality

Date:

- What could I do today that would make me feel genuinely happy and content?

- How can I show myself some love today?

- In what ways did I love myself today?

- Who did I make happy today?

- Who brings me feelings of joy and happiness?

- Who do I truly love?

- What is the smallest step I can take today that will take me a bit closer to my greatest dream?

Reflection Time
Scripting My New Reality

Date:

- What could I do today that would make me feel genuinely happy and content?

- How can I show myself some love today?

- In what ways did I love myself today?

- Who did I make happy today?

- Who brings me feelings of joy and happiness?

- Who do I truly love?

- What is the smallest step I can take today that will take me a bit closer to my greatest dream?

Reflection Time
Scripting My New Reality

Date:

- What could I do today that would make me feel genuinely happy and content?

- How can I show myself some love today?

- In what ways did I love myself today?

- Who did I make happy today?

- Who brings me feelings of joy and happiness?

- Who do I truly love?

- What is the smallest step I can take today that will take me a bit closer to my greatest dream?

Reflection Time
Scripting My New Reality

Date:

- What could I do today that would make me feel genuinely happy and content?

- How can I show myself some love today?

- In what ways did I love myself today?

- Who did I make happy today?

- Who brings me feelings of joy and happiness?

- Who do I truly love?

- What is the smallest step I can take today that will take me a bit closer to my greatest dream?

Reflection Time
Scripting My New Reality

Date:

- What could I do today that would make me feel genuinely happy and content?

- How can I show myself some love today?

- In what ways did I love myself today?

- Who did I make happy today?

- Who brings me feelings of joy and happiness?

- Who do I truly love?

- What is the smallest step I can take today that will take me a bit closer to my greatest dream?

Reflection Time
Scripting My New Reality

Date:

- What could I do today that would make me feel genuinely happy and content?

- How can I show myself some love today?

- In what ways did I love myself today?

- Who did I make happy today?

- Who brings me feelings of joy and happiness?

- Who do I truly love?

- What is the smallest step I can take today that will take me a bit closer to my greatest dream?

Reflection Time
Scripting My New Reality

Date:

- What could I do today that would make me feel genuinely happy and content?

- How can I show myself some love today?

- In what ways did I love myself today?

- Who did I make happy today?

- Who brings me feelings of joy and happiness?

- Who do I truly love?

- What is the smallest step I can take today that will take me a bit closer to my greatest dream?

Reflection Time
Scripting My New Reality

Date:

- What could I do today that would make me feel genuinely happy and content?

- How can I show myself some love today?

- In what ways did I love myself today?

- Who did I make happy today?

- Who brings me feelings of joy and happiness?

- Who do I truly love?

- What is the smallest step I can take today that will take me a bit closer to my greatest dream?

Reflection Time
Scripting My New Reality

Date:

- What could I do today that would make me feel genuinely happy and content?

- How can I show myself some love today?

- In what ways did I love myself today?

- Who did I make happy today?

- Who brings me feelings of joy and happiness?

- Who do I truly love?

- What is the smallest step I can take today that will take me a bit closer to my greatest dream?

Reflection Time
Scripting My New Reality

Date:

- What could I do today that would make me feel genuinely happy and content?

- How can I show myself some love today?

- In what ways did I love myself today?

- Who did I make happy today?

- Who brings me feelings of joy and happiness?

- Who do I truly love?

- What is the smallest step I can take today that will take me a bit closer to my greatest dream?

Reflection Time
Scripting My New Reality

Date:

- What could I do today that would make me feel genuinely happy and content?

- How can I show myself some love today?

- In what ways did I love myself today?

- Who did I make happy today?

- Who brings me feelings of joy and happiness?

- Who do I truly love?

- What is the smallest step I can take today that will take me a bit closer to my greatest dream?

Reflection Time
Scripting My New Reality

Date:

- What could I do today that would make me feel genuinely happy and content?

- How can I show myself some love today?

- In what ways did I love myself today?

- Who did I make happy today?

- Who brings me feelings of joy and happiness?

- Who do I truly love?

- What is the smallest step I can take today that will take me a bit closer to my greatest dream?

Reflection Time
Scripting My New Reality

Date:

- What could I do today that would make me feel genuinely happy and content?

- How can I show myself some love today?

- In what ways did I love myself today?

- Who did I make happy today?

- Who brings me feelings of joy and happiness?

- Who do I truly love?

- What is the smallest step I can take today that will take me a bit closer to my greatest dream?

Reflection Time
Scripting My New Reality

Date:

- What could I do today that would make me feel genuinely happy and content?

- How can I show myself some love today?

- In what ways did I love myself today?

- Who did I make happy today?

- Who brings me feelings of joy and happiness?

- Who do I truly love?

- What is the smallest step I can take today that will take me a bit closer to my greatest dream?

Reflection Time
Scripting My New Reality

Date:

- What could I do today that would make me feel genuinely happy and content?

- How can I show myself some love today?

- In what ways did I love myself today?

- Who did I make happy today?

- Who brings me feelings of joy and happiness?

- Who do I truly love?

- What is the smallest step I can take today that will take me a bit closer to my greatest dream?

Reflection Time
Scripting My New Reality

Date:

- What could I do today that would make me feel genuinely happy and content?

- How can I show myself some love today?

- In what ways did I love myself today?

- Who did I make happy today?

- Who brings me feelings of joy and happiness?

- Who do I truly love?

- What is the smallest step I can take today that will take me a bit closer to my greatest dream?

Reflection Time
Scripting My New Reality

Date:

- What could I do today that would make me feel genuinely happy and content?

- How can I show myself some love today?

- In what ways did I love myself today?

- Who did I make happy today?

- Who brings me feelings of joy and happiness?

- Who do I truly love?

- What is the smallest step I can take today that will take me a bit closer to my greatest dream?

Reflection Time
Scripting My New Reality

Date:

- What could I do today that would make me feel genuinely happy and content?

- How can I show myself some love today?

- In what ways did I love myself today?

- Who did I make happy today?

- Who brings me feelings of joy and happiness?

- Who do I truly love?

- What is the smallest step I can take today that will take me a bit closer to my greatest dream?

Reflection Time
Scripting My New Reality

Date:

- What could I do today that would make me feel genuinely happy and content?

- How can I show myself some love today?

- In what ways did I love myself today?

- Who did I make happy today?

- Who brings me feelings of joy and happiness?

- Who do I truly love?

- What is the smallest step I can take today that will take me a bit closer to my greatest dream?

Reflection Time
Scripting My New Reality

Date:

- What could I do today that would make me feel genuinely happy and content?

- How can I show myself some love today?

- In what ways did I love myself today?

- Who did I make happy today?

- Who brings me feelings of joy and happiness?

- Who do I truly love?

- What is the smallest step I can take today that will take me a bit closer to my greatest dream?

Reflection Time
Scripting My New Reality

Date:

- What could I do today that would make me feel genuinely happy and content?

- How can I show myself some love today?

- In what ways did I love myself today?

- Who did I make happy today?

- Who brings me feelings of joy and happiness?

- Who do I truly love?

- What is the smallest step I can take today that will take me a bit closer to my greatest dream?

Reflection Time
Scripting My New Reality

Date:

- What could I do today that would make me feel genuinely happy and content?

- How can I show myself some love today?

- In what ways did I love myself today?

- Who did I make happy today?

- Who brings me feelings of joy and happiness?

- Who do I truly love?

- What is the smallest step I can take today that will take me a bit closer to my greatest dream?

Reflection Time
Scripting My New Reality

Date:

- What could I do today that would make me feel genuinely happy and content?

- How can I show myself some love today?

- In what ways did I love myself today?

- Who did I make happy today?

- Who brings me feelings of joy and happiness?

- Who do I truly love?

- What is the smallest step I can take today that will take me a bit closer to my greatest dream?

Reflection Time
Scripting My New Reality

Date:

- What could I do today that would make me feel genuinely happy and content?

- How can I show myself some love today?

- In what ways did I love myself today?

- Who did I make happy today?

- Who brings me feelings of joy and happiness?

- Who do I truly love?

- What is the smallest step I can take today that will take me a bit closer to my greatest dream?

Reflection Time
Scripting My New Reality

Date:

- What could I do today that would make me feel genuinely happy and content?

- How can I show myself some love today?

- In what ways did I love myself today?

- Who did I make happy today?

- Who brings me feelings of joy and happiness?

- Who do I truly love?

- What is the smallest step I can take today that will take me a bit closer to my greatest dream?

Reflection Time
Scripting My New Reality

Date:

- What could I do today that would make me feel genuinely happy and content?

- How can I show myself some love today?

- In what ways did I love myself today?

- Who did I make happy today?

- Who brings me feelings of joy and happiness?

- Who do I truly love?

- What is the smallest step I can take today that will take me a bit closer to my greatest dream?

Reflection Time
Scripting My New Reality

Date:

- What could I do today that would make me feel genuinely happy and content?

- How can I show myself some love today?

- In what ways did I love myself today?

- Who did I make happy today?

- Who brings me feelings of joy and happiness?

- Who do I truly love?

- What is the smallest step I can take today that will take me a bit closer to my greatest dream?

Reflection Time
Scripting My New Reality

Date:

- What could I do today that would make me feel genuinely happy and content?

- How can I show myself some love today?

- In what ways did I love myself today?

- Who did I make happy today?

- Who brings me feelings of joy and happiness?

- Who do I truly love?

- What is the smallest step I can take today that will take me a bit closer to my greatest dream?

Reflection Time
Scripting My New Reality

Date:

- What could I do today that would make me feel genuinely happy and content?

- How can I show myself some love today?

- In what ways did I love myself today?

- Who did I make happy today?

- Who brings me feelings of joy and happiness?

- Who do I truly love?

- What is the smallest step I can take today that will take me a bit closer to my greatest dream?

Reflection Time
Scripting My New Reality

Date:

- What could I do today that would make me feel genuinely happy and content?

- How can I show myself some love today?

- In what ways did I love myself today?

- Who did I make happy today?

- Who brings me feelings of joy and happiness?

- Who do I truly love?

- What is the smallest step I can take today that will take me a bit closer to my greatest dream?

Reflection Time
Scripting My New Reality

Date:

- What could I do today that would make me feel genuinely happy and content?

- How can I show myself some love today?

- In what ways did I love myself today?

- Who did I make happy today?

- Who brings me feelings of joy and happiness?

- Who do I truly love?

- What is the smallest step I can take today that will take me a bit closer to my greatest dream?

Reflection Time
Scripting My New Reality

Date:

- What could I do today that would make me feel genuinely happy and content?

- How can I show myself some love today?

- In what ways did I love myself today?

- Who did I make happy today?

- Who brings me feelings of joy and happiness?

- Who do I truly love?

- What is the smallest step I can take today that will take me a bit closer to my greatest dream?

Reflection Time
Scripting My New Reality

Date:

- What could I do today that would make me feel genuinely happy and content?

- How can I show myself some love today?

- In what ways did I love myself today?

- Who did I make happy today?

- Who brings me feelings of joy and happiness?

- Who do I truly love?

- What is the smallest step I can take today that will take me a bit closer to my greatest dream?

Reflection Time
Scripting My New Reality

Date:

- What could I do today that would make me feel genuinely happy and content?

- How can I show myself some love today?

- In what ways did I love myself today?

- Who did I make happy today?

- Who brings me feelings of joy and happiness?

- Who do I truly love?

- What is the smallest step I can take today that will take me a bit closer to my greatest dream?

References

- 5 ways to raise your vibration and have more positive energy. (2017, June 26). Follow Your Own Rhythm. https://www.followyourownrhythm.com/blog-1/2017/6/18/5-ways-to-raise-yo
- 20 powerful positive affirmations. (2020, May 28). Living With Tessa.
- 65 Powerful Affirmations for Self-Love & Healing. (n/d). A Point of Light. https://apointoflight.co/affirmations-for-self-love/
- Aida, K. (2016, November 22). How to Speak Your Dreams Into Existence (With the Law of Attraction). Kelsey Aida. https://kelseyaida.com/theinspirationalblog/how-to-speak-your-dreams-into-existence-law-of-attraction?format=amp
- A Beginner's Guide to the Law of Attraction: Part One. (n/d). Lucky Love Life.https://www.luckylovelife.com/2018/01/04/beginners-guide-law-attraction-part-one/-vibration-and-have-more-positive-energy
- Fox, M. (n/d). Inspired Action is Key to Your Manifestation Success. Self-Made Ladies. https://selfmadeladies.com/inspired-action-key-
- Gange, D. (2020, May 18). The Law of Attraction The 10 Universal Laws To Live By. Do Law of Attraction. https://dolawofattraction.com/the-law-of-attraction-the-10-universal-laws-to-live-by
- How to manifest your dreams into reality: 6 Helpful Tips for Everybody. Meditation Brain Waves. https://meditationbrainwaves.com/how-to-manifest-your-dreams-into-reality/
- Law of Attraction Scripting: 7 Easy Exercises to Manifest Your Dream Life. (n/d). The Path Provides. https://www.thepathprovides.com/blog/7-easy-scripting-exercises-successfully-use-the-law-of-attraction-to-manifest-the-life-you-want
- Manifesting Rituals to Help Manifest Your Dreams Into Reality. (n/d). Meditation Brain Waves. https://meditationbrainwaves.com/manifesting-rituals/

- Manifestation Techniques [14 Powerful Ways to Achieve Your Dreams]. (n/d). Meditation Brain Waves. https://meditationbrainwaves.com/manifestation-techniques/
- Ritlop, R. (2021, May 5). How To Set Intentions For Manifesting. The Confused Millennial.https://www.theconfusedmillennial.com/set-intentions-manifesting/https://www.livingwithtessa.com/20-positive-affirmations-to-use-every-day/
- Young, A. (n/d). How to become a vibrational match to your desire. Subconscious Servant. https://subconsciousservant.com/how-to-become-a-vibrational-match-to-your-desire

Books In This Series: A New Leaf

Everyone and anyone deserves to live a better life beyond their wildest dreams. Understand that life is not perfect, but it is you that can change and better your life.

Transform your emotions, feelings, and habits to the lifestyle that makes you happy.

Habits That Changed Everything

Find out your potential to unlock yourself from bad habits to good habits. Recite your daily affirmation on the changes you like to make and work towards those goals.

Join the author for a first-person journey to a better, happier life, driven by self-love and the good habits that change everything.
https://www.amazon.com/gp/product/B09JK8JJ7J

Self Love Agreements

How can you love others when you don't love yourself?

Love yourself first before you love anything else. Self-love is about caring for yourself first (your health, emotions, habits, happiness, etc) before you care about others.
Self-love is not about selfishness, but the habit of living a happy life through self-compassion.

In this book, there are eight self-love agreements that pave the journey to self-love.
https://www.amazon.com/gp/product/B09JK7W5C5

33 Rules For Life - Master Your Emotions

The wise man has no rules for he has learned and followed the rules of his own life. Life is never easy, some may say. However, the wise man knows that everything is temporality. Everything is interconnected.

Emotionally, he does not care from his mind, but from his heart. He is in sync with 'The One', and The Universal Law. To live a happy life, he has mastered his emotions to achieve ultimate wisdom and gratitude.
https://www.amazon.com/gp/product/B09LT8BKJ9

Daily Manifestation Journal For Men & Women

How can I receive abundance and good luck in my life?

To manifest abundance in our lives, we need to have faith in the Universal Laws. In this book, you shall learn about the law of attraction, how to create a positive mindset, how to master your emotions and feelings, and using the art of gratitude to boost manifestations.

This book includes daily affirmation exercises and tools to attract love, wealth, happiness, and abundance.

About the author

A retired professor, Leslie Leong has taught at a number of universities in the U.S.A., and in the U.K.

Leslie has always been interested to guide and mentor young adults to better improve their lives in various aspects. It is apparent that soft skills make a primary difference in our daily lives.

While in academia, Leslie has been recognized and nominated by the students on several occasions for the teaching excellence awards.

Leslie has traveled extensively around the world and has learned that respect and interacting with people form the basis of harmonious relationships in life.

In Collaboration:
We enjoy writing and publishing books that help people find happiness in their lives. Our independently published books are related to personal experiences of ourselves and others. People seem to be striving in life and life journey can be daunting to some. That's not the way to living. It is never too late to change our lives.

We do not believe that successful people find happiness. We believe that when happiness is found, success follows.

Made in the USA
Monee, IL
11 April 2022